Never Expected

Never Expected

Principles for Living

Dr. Charles Frangella

Copyright © 2019 Dr. Charles Frangella.

All rights reserved. No part of this book may be used or reproduced by any means, graphic, electronic, or mechanical, including photocopying, recording, taping or by any information storage retrieval system without the written permission of the author except in the case of brief quotations embodied in critical articles and reviews.

This book is a work of non-fiction. Unless otherwise noted, the author and the publisher make no explicit guarantees as to the accuracy of the information contained in this book and in some cases, names of people and places have been altered to protect their privacy.

Archway Publishing books may be ordered through booksellers or by contacting:

Archway Publishing
1663 Liberty Drive
Bloomington, IN 47403
www.archwaypublishing.com
1 (888) 242-5904

Because of the dynamic nature of the Internet, any web addresses or links contained in this book may have changed since publication and may no longer be valid. The views expressed in this work are solely those of the author and do not necessarily reflect the views of the publisher, and the publisher hereby disclaims any responsibility for them.

Any people depicted in stock imagery provided by Getty Images are models, and such images are being used for illustrative purposes only. Certain stock imagery © Getty Images.

Cover photo provided by Ed's Photogenics, Ripley, WV.

Scripture taken from the New King James Version. Copyright © 1979, 1980, 1982 by Thomas Nelson, Inc. Used by permission. All rights reserved.

Scripture taken from the King James Version of the Bible.

ISBN: 978-1-4808-8024-5 (sc)
ISBN: 978-1-4808-8025-2 (hc)
ISBN: 978-1-4808-8024-5 (e)

Library of Congress Control Number: 2019912552

Print information available on the last page.

Archway Publishing rev. date: 9/11/2019

CONTENTS

Preface vii

Acknowledgments xi

CHAPTER 1   Serious about the Seriousness of
the Moment 1

CHAPTER 2   Finally It's Not the Bottom Line 9

CHAPTER 3   The Power of Little 19

CHAPTER 4   and the Difference Is! 27

CHAPTER 5   Aimless 37

CHAPTER 6   If It's Broken, It May Never Mend 45

CHAPTER 7   Just Keep Yelling! 53

CHAPTER 8   I Didn't Get It. I Can't Have It. I
Want It Now! 61

CHAPTER 9   How Much Longer Until We Get There? 77

CHAPTER 10   Success: Where Is It? And How Do
I Get It? 83

CHAPTER 11   "I Have No Silver or Gold, But
What I Have I Give" 93

CHAPTER 12   "Without It, We Would Be Most
Miserable" 101

PREFACE

AS THE SUN RISES EVERY MORNING AND interrupts the darkness, so often does a brief moment of enlightenment interrupt life. A short statement, a quip, or a word that is completely never expected can all shed light on a moment of darkness or complacency. In an instant, the light can expose years of misunderstandings, naïveté, and ignorance. That one moment may be simply something that is unique to the incident or that you had heard countless times through your life, but it never had quite the revelation or impact as at the present.

In that moment, you may receive a principle that can help you navigate the treacherous rapids or the peaceful waters of everyday life. Like turning the light on when you come into a room, you instantly can see every potential hazard and possible comfort and then know exactly what you must do to navigate to the other side. We need to learn to embrace those moments of light and accept all that they have for us.

I have been blessed to have traveled with some of the most diversified and high-profile people as well as some of the most common and untraveled people in the world. I have found that, regardless of where they come from, a never-expected moment can bring some of the most interesting, valuable, and applicable principles for living.

In the book you are about to read, I hope you will see that this is just the way that we receive principles in life. They come through the subtlest interruptions that are never expected. The ever-important design in life is to make a break in the flow of events, to single out the importance of the life principle, perhaps even the principal chosen to deliver it.

I want to convey this caution: do not approach this endeavor with a host full of preconceived ideas that good valuable principles can only come from the infinite wise and most noted people of the ages. I implore you that they can come from a myriad of people. True wisdom is indiscriminate. It just makes itself known when it is necessary, not convenient. It almost always is an interruption, a never-expected thing, not a convenient, well-planned, personal effort to better one's self. It is literally, as I stated, like the sunrise coming up, putting an end to an exceptional dark night.

I hope you will accept that the people I mention are individuals I have been around, interacted with, and gleaned in a most unassuming way. These *principals,* (individuals) have knowingly and unknowingly given *principles* (a basic rule or standard) or nuggets for living that have been life-changing, not just academic. These principals have given me principles. It is important to know that the names I reference are to give them credit where credit is due. It is not to laud over their accomplishments, give notoriety, be a name-dropper for some type of self-serving accolade, or impress you of my connections in life.

Instead it is to point to the everyday, casual, and impactful way that principals divinely implanted in our life's path change our lives. We need to notice and embrace the wisdom that is dropped (unexpectedly) upon us from them. If we will only understand that it is because of our life and not in spite of it, we will be better for it.

Some of the inspiration for approaching a manuscript of this nature was to share with the reader principles that have proven themselves with positive and lasting results, ones, let's say, that have passed through the fire and ones you can count on over and over through hard, bad, good, and all times. I daresay they are principles that can change your perspective, approach, walk, relationships, and life.

I have tried to present each principle in the setting in which I received it. I wanted to clothe it in the subtlety of the impact and surprise of the moment. That's how life is. It never really comes knocking on the door, saying, "Here I am! It's time to be bowled over by life's interruption and get smart and grow." So each chapter embodies the person and his or her profoundness and the setting in which I had my casual, subtle moment that changed my life.

The interpretation of the principles I am going to share are mine. The person passing on his or her principle may have had a different meaning in mind, but the way it impacted me, and how I decided to apply it to my life are specific to me. They are not responsible for my interpretation or application. As you read this book, you too may have your own application and interpretation. That's how truth works.

The essence of the truth is unchangeable, but the impact and application are truly unique to its user. Hopefully as you read these chapters, you will seize some of the principles and make them some of the ingredients for your life. Some may be very familiar; others you may have never heard before. What I hope is you will have a new interpretation and application of a principle for living that was "never expected."

Let's get started!

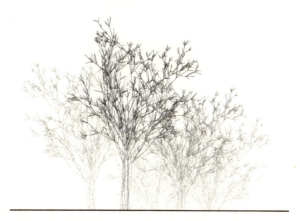

ACKNOWLEDGMENTS

All my gratitude goes to my wife, Marcia, who has helped by being supportive in this totally unknown adventure. I want to thank Sambra Kinder Frangella for helping with the editing during a most difficult time in her life. Thanks also to all of those people that God so graciously put into my life and gave me principles for living. That I never expected.

CHAPTER 1

Serious about the Seriousness of the Moment

*The best time to open
a gift is the present.*

IT WAS A CASUAL ACQUAINTANCE. HE was a new university president who had just moved from a wealthy area in southern California, where he had been the senior pastor of a very fast-growing church. I was a few years younger and had just moved across the country to continue graduate studies in this highly esteemed school. I was a former missionary, businessman, and now the new president of the graduate class.

Passing in the hall one day, I asked this tall, young,

dynamic college president if he would meet me for lunch at his convenience. To my amazement, he agreed, and we wasted no time to set a date, time, and place. That was Joe. He made every moment count. I always felt important around him and knew that every minute was precious.

On the given day, we met and began a usual getting-to-know-you conversation.

"How are you?"

"Tell me about yourself."

And so on. I was quite taken aback on his down-to-earth way.

As we each threw out bits of conversation, he tried to keep things on an easy level, and I continually attempted to come up with something sensational to say. I kept thinking, *"I have never really tried to impress anyone."* That was not me. I was not that trite, yet Joe was the kind of person who just made everyone, want to be better. You never wanted to just get by when you were around him. You always wanted to give your best. But I was relaxed, and as we conversed, I found myself talking about a sales manager that I had known some years before.

As I began to share a piece of wisdom that I thought was enlightening to me, I saw Joe unravel the napkin from the silverware and begin to write. I thought for a moment while I was still speaking, *He must not be interested. Perhaps some school business crossed his mind, and maybe he is evaluating me.* I decided to stop talking and wait for him to finish.

Suddenly he stopped and said, "Keep going. This is good stuff."

I replied, "You sure? I didn't want to interrupt your thought."

He answered, "No, I am writing down what you are saying. I didn't want to forget it."

That's impressive. It's a life lesson. I have a university president, a PhD, a former mega church pastor, and an accomplished author and a successful person thinking I have something to say. I had never felt so important or impressed with another person.

George Washington Carver, a genius scientist from the late 1800s and early 1900s, (also a personal hero of mine) was once asked, "What is the best advice you can give someone?"

He replied, "Do the best you can with what you have and do it now."

Wow! Most people get the first part, "Do the best you can." Doing the best with what you have is a little stretch for many. Most people don't want to work with just what they have. They want something extra or radically different before they make a move. The whole concept is often simply reduced to "taking care of business." That way, the idea sounds easier, attainable, and cute. People have it written on their T-shirts, engraved on plaques on their desks, and even wear carved-out letters that hang on a gold neck chain.

It is "give it your best." There is neither a reduced effort nor an unfocused approach. Just give it your best shot. Make this effort with what you have. Don't make excuses, such as "I don't have what I need" or "Give me what anybody else needs."

Just use what you have. It is the last part though that is so important. Now! Do it now! Timing is the importance. Don't procrastinate. Don't try to over think the issue. Don't over analyze it. Sometimes you have to react. You have to grab the moment.

How many times have you had a great idea, heard a brilliant statement, or gotten an inspiration for some significant move in your life and then sat and did nothing? You kept thinking, *I don't have what I need* or *I'm not in the right position*. Or perhaps you think you need more time. You lost the moment.

Later you tried to remember what it was, and you could only recall fragments of the original idea or nothing at all. How many times have you waited, only to have circumstances change and the opportunity lost? How many times have you decided to implement your belated brilliance, but the wasted time allowed so much criticism and negativity to creep in that you lost the excitement and the creativity?

You have to unravel the silverware, grab the napkin, and write. You have to stop all interruptions and say, "Keep going." It is for you and the other person.

Joe got inspired and educated. I got inspired and rewarded. Doing the best you can with what you have is good. But we are all left with that end. We all work with what we have. We don't always do the best with it, but most of us try. After all, what else can we do with what we have? Ah! But to do it now is the game changer. The person who moves and does so significantly is the one who accomplishes and is rewarded. "Now" brings the results and the blessings. "Now" makes your idea the first one that everyone remembers. Now is the first and lasting impression.

I once worked on a concrete crew. We did poured concrete walls and other types of concrete work. I was forming and pouring a wall one day when I learned the now of importance. As we were pouring a four-foot-tall wall and moving around a corner to begin working on the back portion, we heard a great thud. We immediately looked to the source of the sound and saw the wall we had just poured laying on the ground.

The boss had been sitting on a dozer just beyond the area that had been poured. A shovel was leaning against the blade of the dozer. By the time we had turned around, he came off the dozer, grabbed the shovel on his way down, and began cleaning off the concrete forms that had fallen.

There was no guessing, no analyzing, and no contemplating about the best course to take. There was just "do the best I can with what I have, and do it now!"

In a few minutes we had the forms cleaned, reset, and poured once again. The crisis was over, and we could go on to the next phase. That is the now. Whether it is crisis, a moment of brilliance, or inspiration, the now is the difference.

The next truth that came out of our meeting is humility. Joe, the university president, was humble enough to grab truth in any circumstance. He didn't care that I was just a student. He was willing to immediately accept the lunch invitation and then open his mind to any truth he could glean from the encounter. When he was planning to come to lunch that day, I had no doubt he was thinking, *What can I learn from this guy I'm about to meet?*

His approach to life was to make every moment count and to take truth from wherever it comes. To have that approach, one has to be humble with no pretense. Truth is not biased, racist, or prejudiced. It is simply truth. It will smack you in the face, and if you don't grab it while you can, after it beats you up with simplicity and profoundness, it will move on. The person who knows this, understands, as did Joe Aldrich (Multnomah University President), and George Washington Carver, to not let arrogance, pride, or selfishness steal his or her opportunity for improvement.

(What was I telling Joe that he was writing down? "First impressions are made within the first ten seconds of a meeting." I just thought you might want to know.)

CHAPTER 2

Finally It's Not the Bottom Line

The fall was really exciting, but the sudden stop was a killer.

THE ONE THING THAT PLAGUES A PERSON when they are in business is a phrase, the "bottom line." It seems once the person goes into their dream idea and begins building, creating, producing, or making their "self-proposed" brilliance known to the world, they are hit with the reality of the bottom line. This accounting term refers to one's balance sheet or other financial document. It also refers to the underlying or ultimate outcome or criterion.

Over time it has become a euphemism to mean the end of something or to get to the finish, final stop, and so on.

The bottom line is actually not any of those things. It is simply an accounting term to express the conclusion that one needs to reach to make a profit. Any other conclusion and one has to work at changing the bottom line.

This phrase usually begins to haunt every business owner, manager, chief executive officer, and chief financial officer. Suddenly one goal motivates every business, to produce a better product, make a happier customer, create something safe for the environment, and so forth.

LOL! LOL! LOL! You have got to be kidding. It is none of those things. It is the bottom line, the margin of profit, or the "what's left." Everything done in the company has to meet one criterion, to make the bottom line profitable.

When I first went into business, I was nineteen. I started a company selling a soap product that was a very good commodity but a very hard sell. At first the excitement was overwhelming. Eventually though, the reality of paying for products, helpers, and, of course, taxes arose. That's when the bottom line hit me.

Wow! Do you mean all of that money was not mine? What happened? The euphemistic phrase became a nightmare. It pushed, pulled, shoved, twisted, weighted, crushed, and demoralized me until I couldn't take it anymore. What had happened to all those dreams I saw in other people who were self-employed? They seemed to have so much happiness. Was business that much of a problem? It seemed that way for some time.

A few years later, though, I tried again. I went into my dream world with a different attitude. My endeavors, now housed in a new approach, paid off. However, that enigmatic phrase still relentlessly hounded me. Now, however, I could bear it with a little more tolerance.

Here is the kicker. There is a principle that if applied along the way can make not only business but life itself profitable and still retain the quality. If I fast-forward about ten years, there is an epiphany about to take place in my life that will illustrate my point.

I entered graduate school and was thrown into an environment of high-level scholastics, hard-driven professors, and extremely nitpicking advisors .It was a relentless atmosphere that took a lot of adjusting.

My first encounter was an advisor who no other student seemed to want, so I volunteered. I thought, *Maybe this guy could help me with my much-needed adjustment and my lack of discipline.* Be careful what you ask for. You just might get it!

About two months into the program, I had a deadline to turn in a draft of the introduction and first chapter of my proposed thesis. Proudly, I headed to my advisor's office, left my literary treasure, and headed back home.

The next day I got a call from his office with a request to stop in that afternoon. It's funny how some things stick in your mind and seem to never leave you. It was a beautiful, sunny day. The air had a hint of autumn in it, and I was feeling like I could conquer the world. Get ready!

I stopped in the administration building, went into his office, and sat down. He said to me as he handed me my paper, "You need to bring everything to its *irreducible minimum.*"

Opening my paper, I was so shocked that I had a delayed reaction to his statement. As I looked at my paper and saw nothing but red marks all over every page, I could barely get my breath back.

"What did I do wrong?" I thought.

Of course the first reaction is to defend what you have done and why it should be the way you wrote it. Yes, that is exactly what I did.

After all, I thought, *I have been a successful business- man and a college graduate, and this is not my first rodeo.* None of that mattered. What mattered was that it was not a good beginning to a research paper that was going to take a year to complete and be the measuring device that would determine my graduation.

"Uh, what did you say?" I stammered.

The answer came back. "You need to bring everything to its *irreducible minimum.*"

NEVER EXPECTED

There it was again. *What is that?* I thought. You know I was not about to ask him. So we talked awhile, and he gave me some direction on what to do to correct the paper. Then I went on my way, straight to the library to find out what in the world did that stupid phrase, that I had never heard before, mean.

Well, it wasn't found in the library, but it was found in life. I went for several years trying to treat it like it was the bottom line. It's not!

Irreducible minimum is a much more complete concept than bottom line. With the bottom line, you can make changes, corrections, and adjustments to alter the outcome to get the bottom line you want. When you bring something or anything to its irreducible, it is as far as you can go. It is brought to a certain condition or form that is reduced or simplified to its completeness. There is no longer any altercation. It is finished, final, and complete.

When you add minimum to the mix and come out with irreducible minimum, you are exhausting any residue that might be overlooked. You are, in addition, decreasing the possibility change so small that, if you go any farther, the item will go from being decreased to being increased. You might say "to the point of no return."

It is not a phrase that is used in business, sports, politics, and so on. It is not often heard anywhere or heard at all, unless you are in a math class. Yes, that's where I remembered it. I had to do a paradigm shift and see it in a different context. Learning how to apply it in more everyday life has been an amazing principle for living. When you begin to put that principle to use in the aforementioned—business, sports, politics, news, and so forth—you find how to add completeness where finality is often lost or disregarded regularly.

When the advisor introduced that interruption into my day, it immediately shed light into my thinking. What he wanted to do was to get me to think more critically. I needed to stop filtering everything through my biases, emotions, and prejudices and look at facts and truth, which is not an easy thing to accomplish.

We grow up believing in fairy tales, ideals, and legends. That is wonderful for children because it helps them to develop their imaginations, and properly guided, they will make the transition from childhood to adulthood just fine. Being a kid is great and necessary. Staying a kid is quite a different matter. The problem becomes that we can grow up believing the old adage, "When the legend becomes fact, print the legend."

It sounds romantic and somewhat noble, but here in the real world, it's not that way. If we don't bring things to their irreducible minimum, we will begin to turn the legend into the truth and begin to believe it.

News that has today become opinion is probably

one of the most frustrating areas that tend to turn legend into truth. Often in the opinion category, a story is never reduced to its irreducible minimum because that cuts the story too short and brings it to conclusion. Conclusion is not the goal, but keeping their subscribers on the hook is.

So the story editor tends to not make the journalist cut away the pork and bring the story to an irreducible minimum, but instead publish the pork and hide the truth as long as possible. When this happens, the listener gets the bias, prejudice, and emotion, but not the completed truth.

In politics, it usually isn't applied because then the opposing side would have to settle too quickly and move on, which pushes the agenda to rely on facts. Facts do not always come into play. They are usually moved to the background to protect a hidden agenda, for example, pork in a bill, an individual or party bias, or a future campaign strategy. Once proposals are brought to their irreducible minimum, the truth is exposed, and all chaos is brought to a close.

Now I must be considerate and not blame those individuals in the previous examples. Let me explain that it is not necessarily due to the people in those venues but, more importantly, to the evolution of our society. The systems in both of those categories are the main problem. News, ideas, and concepts over the decades have changed. Politics are constantly evolving, and the push is against cultural change and time.

The other variant that has introduced itself into the mix is social media. In a matter of a few short years, social media has brought the average person to the national and world stage. Today any individual can voice their opinion, observation, or accusation and instantly broadcast it to the world and have the potential of millions of responses. Suddenly opinion, emotion, or accusation dictates the response without the shred of evidence or fact. The rush to judgment is ramped up, and the sorting out to get to the truth becomes laborious and expensive, with a certain amount of collateral damage that can never be repaired. This has brought not only a need for quick adjustment to fix the problem, but it has put a great distance between chaos and the irreducible minimum.

To bring things to their irreducible minimum is to settle on three things: facts; willingness to accept facts and the change they bring; and inclination to apply the facts, even to your own hurt. It's a lesson you have to learn if you are going to do honest research. No matter how much you believe something, make any kind of adjustments, or want it to be different, it is already based on the irreducible minimum, the ultimate and exhaustive final truth.

Any attempt to try to change or go beyond the irreducible minimum will push you to increase or decrease

NEVER EXPECTED

from that final truth. That is, addition begins to add to the confusion of the truth; either by adding to or subtracting from, and your journey has to start all over. This is a truth that we need to learn how to incorporate into our thinking process. It requires effort. You can't be lazy. You must work diligently to develop the process of not adding the "I" to the <u>run</u> toward the irreducible minimum of truth, because it will bring your efforts to <u>ruin</u> the findings.

CHAPTER 3

The Power of Little

Did you know that stressed is just desserts spelled backward?

HAVE YOU EVER BEEN INTENTLY FOcused in a class, trying to catch every word? You know, one of those times when you are studying something you don't really understand but know you have to get it or be lost for the rest of the semester. Well, if you haven't, my hat goes off to you.

I have been in school so many years that I can point to many times that that has happened to me. It has occurred so often that it has become the norm rather than the exception. It seems I always had one of those moments in every semester, probably because I always had a class that was stretching me to my limits.

I had just decided to go back to college and finish my degree. I had quit several years before with only a semester left to graduate and put all of my energy into trying to become a successful businessman. Now after several years and a life-changing moment, I realized the value of not only finishing my degree but changing my major and virtually starting all over again.

There was a small private college just twenty miles from where I was living, and with a limited schedule, I could keep my business and finish my degree in about two years. It was a plan, and it was exciting.

So here I was sitting in a foreign language class the first day. (I had never taken a foreign language class before; in fact I struggled in English all through school.) In walked the professor, a tall, thin fellow who reminded me of the pictures of Ichabod Crane of *Sleepy Hollow* fame. (He became one of my most beloved professors). The class was Konia Greek, and the challenge was daunting.

Well, the class began, and I already knew I couldn't fool around and let my mind wander. The beginning of any language course is to learn the alphabet and then move on to building a vocabulary and ultimately the ever-foreboding syntax. Well, this instructor wanted to spend the first class preparing us for the upcoming struggle. So he wanted to lay out all of the warnings first about the language we were going to be studying. Here comes the bright light of a never expected moment.

He begins by telling us how Konia Greek is different than Modern Greek. He said, "It is full of idioms, and it is critical—absolutely critical—that you pay attention to the prepositions."

Pay attention to the prepositions! I wasn't really sure what a preposition was; let alone how to watch for one. Wow! This was going to be impossible. Well, it wasn't, and I learned what a preposition was. And I actually learned some Greek along the way. I also learned a great deal about our English language.

Now paying attention to the prepositions is the principle here. A preposition is one of the little words in our language. It is a simple word that sometimes appears to be interchangeable with another, but the change can be critical and preventive from being replaced with an alternative, that is, *into* and *in*. We may say that the person came in the room; however, if the person was outside of the room, then we should say he came into the room. The two words are not interchangeable in that example but appear to be. Doing so completely changes the meaning.

Now I know you are wondering, *Is this that important of a principle?* Well, at the time, I too didn't see all that much significance until I got into other areas of life and realized how often people confuse things because they used the wrong prepositions. If I may, let me give you an example that affects all of us.

The Founding Fathers of our country put together two most amazing documents: the Declaration of Independence and the Constitution of the United States of America. The Founding Fathers were in some ways very diametrically opposed to one another, but they knew they had to put their differences aside to accomplish the greater good.

Now these, aforementioned documents, have been around for over 225 years and still have relevance in today's modern world, ever-changing demographics, and political landscape. Now why is that? It is because of the prepositions. Every time things get a little off course, you just have to go to the prepositions.

A few years ago during an election year, one of the former presidents gave a supportive campaign speech for one of the candidates. He is a good orator and had an excellent speech; however, he built the speech around a falsehood. (I am not taking issue with his speech; this is just for illustration.)He pointed out that the people of America needed to get *with* their government. He went on to say that all Americans wanted to know that their government was *with* them.

These were truly inspiring words, and they made for a

NEVER EXPECTED

very stirring speech; however, they are not only incorrect, but they move the listener to go a wrong direction. The problem is that once you interchange prepositions that are truly not interchangeable, you open a new direction that becomes a change in the fundamental foundation of the subject of your message.

First, *with* is not one of the key prepositions in the relationship of Americans and their government. In fact, the Founding Fathers purposely avoided the concept; however, the preposition *with* is a key to the relationship of Americans and other Americans.

During WWII, Americans were *with* their soldiers and *with* fellow American workers. While it was uncommon for women to work in factories and perform other very hard physical labor, gender and class was put aside, and it was American with American for the greater cause. This is not something that can be legislated. It is part of the human spirit. People are *with* one another because of a desire and a will to put aside differences and join together for the common good.

Second, the Founding Fathers, in their brilliance, understood that they did not want a government body to be *with* anyone. This would imply that the government was something separate and of its own. They saw the government quite differently. So when they formed the critical documents, they used different prepositions—*of, by,* and *for*—that would not be interchangeable with any others for their purpose. These three prepositions are quite exclusive and inclusive in their meaning and use.

Of has to do with the origin of the government. It is where everything begins because it refers to possessiveness. The items in reference have to do with the "rights of" the people. Transient, they move through time, space, and circumstance because they are inalienable. This is part of the makeup of the people; they have rights that are unchangeable and intrinsic.

By has to do also with beginning. The population, not the government, originates things. I know today it doesn't seem that way. We are always wondering what the government is going to do and what hoops they are going to make us jump through. But that is clearly not what the Founding Fathers had envisioned.

By, means just that. It is all done *by* the people. Thus, the government is set up so we have co-equal parts of government. The House of Representatives is the direct representative of the population. It is appropriated according to amounts of population so every segment will have equal recognition. The Senate is decided on an equal basis so each state has equal recognition. Then the executive branch has equal authority, which provides a balance to the legislative branch. The third branch, the judicial branch, has a check to the other two by determining if what they are doing is done according to the laws of the land (simply put). It all starts *by* the people.

For is why it is all done. The Founding Fathers knew they wanted a government that was not like a dictatorship, monarchy, or any other type of single-based authority. They set up their new government *for* the benefit of the people, not the benefit for the ruler. They didn't want a *"with"*, because that puts the government on an equal plane with the people. The position they wanted was to put the people in charge for their own benefit. Anything else will soon turn into an oppressive situation. Not at first, but it will eventually, because that is its nature.

The Founding Fathers saw that, from where they were, and they did not want to make the same mistake again. This new government was going to be different; it was going to be *of* the people, *by* the people, and *for* the people. They had had enough of *with* the people. *With* the people always starts out with good intentions because, as people, we are always looking to be taken care of until the caretaker takes over and our liberty is oppressed.

Historically, oppression leads to retaliation, thus the revolution. Revolutions can take place in a country or in the heart of a single individual. It is a form that eventually becomes the scream that "My liberty (autonomy) has been stolen, and I can't take it anymore!" Whenever a government moves to be oppressive, some type of dramatic change becomes the desire of the people. Whenever a government is with the people and the "*of, by,* and *for*" are left out, a revolution is on the horizon.

We need to watch the prepositions. They are little but very powerful. We need to incorporate them into our thinking, behavior, and plans. I thank Dr. Shimpf for that great lesson. I have been careful to pay attention to the little things that can change the world, the prepositions.

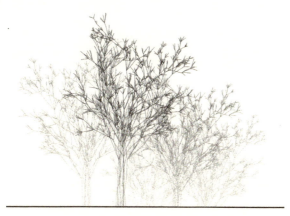

CHAPTER 4
and the Difference Is!

I'm great at multitasking. I can waste time, be unproductive, and procrastinate all at once.

IT WAS A FORTY-MILE DRIVE TO MEET Thomas. He lived about two miles from a little town in West Virginia. He had just purchased a home that had previously belonged to a friend and past business acquaintance of mine, so I knew just where to go. It was an exciting time. He had invited me to be his guest at an important meeting with several dignitaries, for example, a governor's aide, The Mayor of Charleston, heads of the state and local visitors' bureau, and several other key people in the area.

As I arrived with the sun shining, he invited me into his home, and we chatted as he finished up a few final details of business. He then grabbed his keys. We got into his car and headed toward Charleston, about twenty miles away. As we drove down the two-lane road where his home was situated, I began to ask a few probing questions dealing with the upcoming meeting.

He politely explained the seriousness of the meeting, why he asked for it, and what he hoped to accomplish with this next couple of hours. With that out of the way, I proceeded to inquire about him. He is a large man, about six-foot-four and about 250 pounds. He had gone to high school with some people I knew well. I thought that would be a great connection. I immediately went to a person who had graduated the same year he had and was also an outstanding athlete.

"Did you know Mark when you were in high school? He was an outstanding athlete, and his sister was a previous homecoming queen."

My foundation for the question was that I had made a bold assumption, that he had surely been and athlete, having his physique. Thus, the athlete and homecoming queen would be a natural segue into my question.

Before I go any farther with my story, let me fit something in. At times we may think that we are directing a conversation to fit our need when in actuality we are being

NEVER EXPECTED

primed to receive a revolutionary experience that will impact our life, monumentally and eternally. It may be the most simple and direct truth that we would never expect, if we were to investigate it, but because it comes with surprise and subtlety, we are open, ready, and prepared. Not knowingly prepared, but blindsided prepared.

It's that turn of a phrase in a song that you can't get out of your head or the common statement that someone expresses differently than you have ever heard before. There could even be an unusual conclusion that someone draws that you never thought of, which changes the whole perspective of the subject. Once that happens, it seems that that change is always there, and you can never see the same thing again without including that one dynamic view. That was about to happen for me, and I was not, of course, expecting it. Back to the story!

He answered me by saying that he did not play sports in school. He didn't know a lot of athletes and wasn't really all that familiar with who the homecoming queens were. I was taken aback with a long pause before I could even respond. Where do I go? What subject do I switch to, but would that fall short too? I wasn't prepared for his response. How could this very dynamic person be someone who didn't connect with the high-profile things of high school, like homecoming queens and athletes? There was the difference. What I had experienced and what had been important to me was not even close to what he had experienced and what was important to him.

As we drove a little further, it came to me. He was a pastor, so maybe I should pursue that line of questioning. "Were you involved in your church youth group?"

"Yes, some, but I played piano for the church when I was about thirteen."

I didn't expect that answer. I was thinking he would hit me with he was on the debate team or a member of some youth group team.

But he continued his answer. "I have always been a serious person."

What an explosion! He said something simple, but I heard something so profound. Now what he meant and what I heard may be totally different, but I can assure you that that one statement changed my life. To this day and even as I write this, it brings tears and reflections to me.

I'm sure he was not saying you are frivolous or petty if you are an athlete, don't attend church, or aren't interested in who homecoming queen is. That is not what I heard. I didn't hear that you must never laugh, cutup, or enjoy a lighthearted moment. I knew that he wasn't being biased or snobbish. He was simply making a statement about his perspective of life growing up and how to approach things. That's what I heard.

I heard a principle of life, one that is so simple that

NEVER EXPECTED

most people never pay any attention. Most never hear the seriousness of that statement. It is to make every moment have a purpose. Look at the moment and situation and find the purpose.

It has to do with *foundation, perspective, and motivation.* I daresay that I and maybe most of us are slow to shed our youth, youthful ideas, and views as we get older. We, for the most part, take those ideas and drag them along into our adulthood and mix them all up with our adult decisions. We aren't acting silly or juvenile. That would be obvious and necessary to cleanse out of our life choices. What we often do is cling to the building blocks that we used as a youth, incorporate them into our adult foundation, and then try to build a significant structure on them. Let's break these three down.

Foundation

Just as in a building, the weight of everything rests on that structure, which is the interesting part about a foundation. It is not really the depth of the foundation that is the most important part, although it is very significant. The breadth is the real determining factor. The same is true when building a foundation for your life, habits, thoughts, approaches, and conclusions.

When this foundation is built, it must be broadened,

and in the process, some of the unnecessary material must be discarded. Most of us think we can just keep adding and adding to what we already have, and it will be better. Just take youthful ideas and concepts and then add some more mature ideas and concepts. Then we will have a better foundation. In reality, that makes for a bigger, not better, foundation. What we need to do is take what depth comes with maturity and broaden it, not necessarily deepen it. The bigger building needs depth, but more importantly, it needs width or breadth. With width, it has a much wider area to compress, which of course is much more difficult and lends strength and stability.

Perspective

Again the adult-and-child analogy works. Have you ever had a friend when you were a youth who always seemed a little older, reserved, or together? Sometimes they appeared just out of step with everyone else? They were a great person, but they were just plain different, and everyone knew it.

It's like the summer job that you would get and think it was a great source to get some money and have some fun during the summer break. Your friend got a summer job and planned on saving some of his earnings, using some to buy some important items and then spending some on his own whims. It is perspective, youthful spending versus responsible spending. Perspective is the filter that determines importance, direction, and consequence.

That is why teachers, politicians, advisors, religious leaders, coaches, and so forth are always trying to change or adjust our perspective. They want to filter out their importance, alter our direction, and control the outcome. The old adage "knowledge is power" is true; however, the real-life changing power that can completely and permanently change a person is *perspective.*

That is not necessarily wrong; it is sometimes needed. We often need a new perspective. We need to enhance our importance, better define our direction, and improve the consequences. At the same time, embracing the wrong mentor can open the door through an altered perspective that can bring us to devaluation, confused direction, and crippling consequences. Being serious-minded; loads proper perspective in our favor. It doesn't assure us of perfect performance. It assures us of performance to pursue perfection. This will be discussed in a later chapter.

Motivation

"As a man thinks so is he." Likes and dislikes more commonly motivate us. We chase dreams, rainbows, and whims. We are up and down like a wild roller coaster. We let every little thing turn, twist, and move us. Every marketing and advertising agency understands this behavior. Each television or radio program, nonprofit organization, and helpful association builds on human conduct. Stores have all types of impulse items at the checkout counters. Movies are built around action, greed, sex, and power. Every advertiser is building a dream for someone to buy.

How are you motivated? Are you motivated through being serious-minded, or do you let your emotions run away with you? Motivation should be built on a balance of a good foundation, proper perspective, and a little dreaming. You have to acknowledge your emotions.

Emotions are a part of us, but you have to know that they will lie to you convincingly and often. They will tell you that you want something when you know you shouldn't. Emotions will alter our perspective and chip away our foundation, yet we have them and need them.

What a dilemma! It is not whether you use them; it is *how* you use them. Again, you have to filter them and make a determination. Is what I am doing for my project, my family, myself, and others good, or is it just pretty, feels good, and makes me tingle all over? I know there is a time for just raw emotions. Maybe at a party where everyone is laughing, perhaps with friends and family at the beach, and countless others times, you just let your emotions have their way. It is making the distinction of when to listen to

NEVER EXPECTED

your emotions and when to push them back and make a serious-minded decision. That serious-minded part is the difference. That is the motivation.

So that day when **Thomas D. Jakes** said, "I have always been a serious-minded person," I heard a principle for my life and hopefully one you can incorporate in yours. We need to have a properly built firm foundation (it's never too late); a solid, clear, and purposeful perspective; and a sensible, meaningful motivation.

CHAPTER 5

Aimless

A couple of years ago, my therapist told me I had problems letting go of the past.

WE HAD JUST FINISHED DINNER. MY daughter was barely eighteen months old, but already a handful. As I took her into the living room and my wife cleaned the table, I was getting ready to settle in for a quiet, uninterrupted evening. I was in graduate school and didn't get many times when I could just relax. I was often overloaded with studies, work, and other responsibilities. Shamefully, that is the plight of many married graduate students. Everything has a priority, and family usually comes down the list. So when you get a moment, you want to cherish it and hope that life doesn't throw you a curve. But life moves on and does not always listen to your expectations. It did this night.

When I went to the living room with my daughter, the telephone rang. As I answered, the thought went through my mind, *I hope this will be something that will help us and not be some telemarketer.* Little did I know!

"Hello."

"Hello," the caller replied. "This is Joe Aldrich."

Immediately I was stunned. *Why would the president of the university be calling me? Surely I haven't done anything so terrible that the president needs to address it, personally.*

As we began to talk, he started describing a construction project the university was embarking on with their newly expanding publishing company. He began to explain in a little detail about the project, the project manager, and the need for some help in one area of the project.

As I listened, I kept wondering, *"Where is all of this going? Why would he take time out of his busy schedule to call me, a student, and discuss this special need that they were facing with this very expensive endeavor?"*

Then he unloaded the reason for the call. "I want you to oversee this part of the project and get it done."

Of course, I was shocked and humbled. I responded, "What makes you think I can do this? I am a student."

"I know you, and I am sure that you can do this," he replied.

Still overwhelmed by his confidence, I began to discuss the matter. He was persistent, even when I voiced all of my concerns.

Then he threw something out that stopped me cold. "If you aim at nothing, you will hit it every time."

With no way to counter that, I responded, "I will meet you tomorrow at your office."

Aimless! Have you ever seen some shiftless, homeless person who you thought was just wasting his life? Maybe you know someone, perhaps a friend or relative, who appears to have a lot of talent and ability but never seems to go anywhere. He never seems to get past square one. When you talk to him, he always has an excuse as to why he has never moved forward.

As he gives his preponderance of evidence for his stagnation in life, you get the picture that he is just lazy, shiftless, or aimless. The truth is he has learned a debilitating lesson, to aim at nothing and believe that the aiming is all there is.

Today we have a culture that is changing to an aimless society. I say this with great respect for those leaders, educators, and motivators who are doing a tremendous job of trying to get the present and next generations on track to achieve great accomplishments. It is a daunting task with present diminishing returns. The learning curve is being altered with a changing society that pushes the agenda of mediocrity. We have a drive to make everyone a winner as well as everyone a loser. It is to make the target not something but anything. When anything becomes the target, then nothing is the goal.

Nothing is what anybody can hit. You can't miss. You hit nothing every time. You don't have to develop the expertise of aiming. You can be aimless. You can just point and shoot. This mentality eliminates the effort factor. Whatever, happens, happens. There is no need to practice or sacrifice as long as you hit anything.

Herein is the overall problem. From the moment we are born, we have to be competitive. We must develop a drive to make it in this very difficult and demanding world. We are literally born to cry for our needs: food, warmth, love, acceptance, and a host of other things. As we grow and develop, we move into the environment that increases the challenges in life and for life. Someone out there is envious and wants either what you want or wants what you have. They are willing to compete for it. If you don't set some goals, they are going to come along and snatch anything or everything out from under you. I know you are saying about now, "This guy is overstating the importance of this principle."Hear me out! Try to get this perspective.

Some years ago while teaching in a public school system,

NEVER EXPECTED

I began to notice a growing complacency among students, particularly as they got into the secondary grades, ninth through twelfth. I noticed that more and more students weren't making plans for after graduation, had no career plans, and appeared to be rather aimless by not having any goals. I was shocked when I would ask them about what they were hoping to accomplish.

The overwhelming answer was, "I don't know, and it doesn't really matter."

Those are words of hopelessness. There was no fire, no hunger, and no passion beyond today. It was frightening to me to see a generation in such a state. You begin to wonder, *where are we going with future leaders having such an outlook and foundation to launch from?* I began to try and instill a motivation for change. Hey! The principle is, *"If you aim at nothing, you hit it every time."*

I was watching a whole generation beginning to believe that hitting nothing was better than hitting something. The minute we let this type of teaching and belief come into our world, it becomes like a cancer. It begins to consume every facet of our life. Soon nothing has any importance, and suddenly our economy begins to suffer. Next, our leadership goes off target. Then our cultural concepts change. Complacency is the norm, and due diligence is the enemy. Personal responsibility becomes nonexistent, and everybody else is to be blamed for my failures and shortcomings.

Finally we find ourselves halfway down a slippery slope wondering, *how did we get here?* We need to go back to target practice and learn how to aim at something.

Some years ago, I had to do a research paper on suicide for a graduate class I was taking. When it was assigned, I thought it would not be too challenging or rewarding. My naïveté can sometimes be shocking.

I will tell you that it was not only eye-opening, but the findings were more than rewarding and scary. The one statistic that was the most enlightening was that at the time, the United States had the highest rate of suicide among people aged fifteen to twenty-four in the world. Absolutely amazing! How does the most advanced nation in the world have such a statistic?

As I researched, I was enlightened to the fact that this age group faced unprecedented hopelessness. It wasn't that their future was hopeless. It was that they perceived it as hopeless. They had become aimless. Their contemporary world seemed to be aimless. Substance was taken from their purpose in life. Their education was of little to no importance. They saw themselves as having no value and thus no reason to continue. Could this be true in a country where people are desperately trying to migrate from all over the world?

The sad truth is that when there is no goal, no need, and no challenge, hope disappears, and despair follows. When despair sets in, all else begins to be lost. It is imperative that we constantly aim at something. We need to continually polish and hone our skills. We must set our sights, take careful aim, and make the effort.

This principle holds true in all that is done as individuals, government, society, parents, friends, and every other segment of life. Parents need to aim at purpose and design in raising their children. They should never look to some other source as the primary developer of their children. All else should only be supplemental. Schools, Boy Scouts, Girl Scouts, church groups, FAA, and 4H are all good and serve a purpose. They just can't be the target.

In government, our Founding Fathers had every intention for the people to do the aiming of where this country was supposed to go. That is why it is *of*, *by*, and *for* the people. You don't see *with*, as mentioned in an earlier chapter. We, not the government, need to be the marksman. Government is the employee; the people are the employer. The employer does the aiming. The employer has to declare what the target is and then get the employees to help hit the target.

With friends and society, we should be centered on developing these two things: to see the best friendships we can have and to be the strongest society we can have. It is important that we put purpose to our friendships. The objective gives value .The same is true with society. It is important as individuals that we need to aim at specific targets in life. Whether we have close or far targets, we need to be aiming at bull's-eyes.

When you hit the target, it provides a sense of accomplishment, value, and meaning. Greater than those things, it gives finality and closure. It says you can move on to the next goal and not have to look back at a heap of unresolved issues that will keep hanging on to the future. That is, purpose, completion, quality, and value can never be taken away. *Aim at something; don't be aimless.*

CHAPTER 6

If It's Broken, It May Never Mend

When my boss asked me who was the stupid one, me or him? I told him, everyone knows, he doesn't hire stupid people.

STOPPING IN A SMALL TOWN IN THE Ozark Mountains, I was hopeful I could find a store where I could buy a few much-needed items. I was planning on moving to the area and thought this would help me get acquainted with the region. It was mild weather, though it was in February. I wasn't accustomed to this. I was still living in Wheaton, Illinois, but I was going to move to the Ozarks and open a business. I was just twenty-five miles from my destination at the time, and the thought was quite exciting to think of making a major move, opening a business, and starting a whole new chapter in my life. Truthfully, it sounded exciting, but I needed a lot of help and didn't know it. Like many people that age, the road had a curve up ahead, but I didn't care what was around it. All that mattered was where I was at that moment.

In business school, it is taught that you need to have an exit strategy before you start the business. It seems strange that you need to know how to get out before you get in. This principle helps you to see the whole picture of the business you are about to embark on. You need to know ahead of time how you will transition from one phase to the next, whether success or failure motivates it. Along the way, you will need to apply other sound principles that may or may not be learned through a school of academics or one of hard knocks. It is advantageous if you can listen to some seasoned business veterans along the way, who have already been to either school or both. When these people cross your path, be sure to sit up, take notice, and absorb all of the wisdom that they impart.

Eventually I found the store that looked like it would fit my need. It was a place I was not familiar with but looked large enough to probably have plenty of selection of merchandise. I was used to stores such as Ventures, Sears, and Kmart, but this was a little version of those

NEVER EXPECTED

called Wal-Mart, an obvious local brand that didn't have many stores at the time. They were not even known in Springfield, Missouri, the third-largest city in the state, which was forty-five miles away.

I went into the store and began to look around for the few items that I needed. One by one, I began to fill my cart when I noticed a woman dressed with a store uniform shirt talking to an irate customer. As the confrontation got a little heated, I saw another man looking at the same two people I was observing. We both watched, and occasionally the other man and I would look at each other. I thought, *He must be thinking the same thing I am thinking. "The store worker needs to get some help and get this matter resolved."*

As we watched, we could tell the customer was not being completely satisfied. Finally the worker summoned the store manager, and things got straightened out. I soon collected all my items and went to the checkout counter. The man who had been standing in the aisle earlier was now just ahead of me in the lane. He said something to the manager, who was actually checking everyone out.

When I got to the register, I mentioned something to the checkout person about the incident and brought up the man who had just gone ahead of me. I mentioned how he was watching the incident from a distance as I was and that I thought we both were hoping the store worker would call the manager to help.

Suddenly she stopped what she was doing and said, "Well, he is the owner of the store."

The thought astonished me. Immediately I wondered why he hadn't jumped in there and let the customer know he was the owner and, by golly, he would take care of the problem. As I finished checking out, I grabbed my items and headed to the parking lot.

The man from the store was a short distance in front of me when I called out to him. "Hey", "Mister."

He stopped and turned to see who was addressing him. "You're the boy who was in the store."

"Yes," I replied. "I wanted to ask you why you didn't get involved in that incident in the store. The manager said you're the owner."

He simply replied, "Never break the chain of command."

Now that may seem simple, but it truly has some tremendous far-reaching dimensions. For a young man of about twenty-five, that was a foundational principle that I needed to know; however, I did not get the grasp of its power until many years later. It's like any first learned principle: you don't always see all of the ramifications until you use it over and over, and then you begin to see its positives, negatives, and unintended consequences.

But the idea of never breaking the chain of command is a very necessary foundational principle that every person who is going to be in any form of management should learn and learn well. Four things need to be considered about this principle: the negative, the other negative, the positive, and the unintended consequences.

Negative of Breaking the Chain

When those under your authority know how you operate and understand that they cannot operate with confidence because you are always there to remind them of their inadequacies and usurp their authority, they will work in fear, doubt, and worry. Their output will be based on insecurity and mistakes.

Negative of "Not" Breaking the Chain

When you don't break the chain, the one looming problem that can and sometimes does arise is that you and your company may suffer loss. When Sam Walton didn't break into the conversation to bring resolution to the issue, he had to live with the consequence. He may have lost the customer; losing one can affect ten others. He understood the possibility, but he was sure he would have a better manager and clerk when it was over. He put his confidence in his ability to hire the right people, move them into the right position, and then trust his abilities and theirs. In the future, that would, payoff, with better customer relations and more customers.

Positive of Not Breaking the Chain

Part of the positive is part of the negative. You have confidence in yourself and your employees (and your customers). A customer who has become discontented, for whatever reason, usually wants to be addressed with respect and is looking for resolve. If the employee cannot give a satisfactory answer, he is ready for someone with more authority to step in and give a final resolution that can be graciously accepted (barring the completely irate customer who does not have a resolution in mind, but that's another subject). Keeping everything in a line and order accomplishes respect for the customer and their complaint. It also develops respect for the employee and their abilities, your management and their abilities, and your ability.

Unintended Consequences

I surely can't list them all. If I could, you probably wouldn't read the rest of this book! Let me say that some of the unintended consequences would be that your company will run smoother and more efficiently. If you have hired people that will trust you, know that you have confidence in them, and realize that you are there, in the event that they need you, they will give you their best.

Most people like to please. They feel good about themselves and where they are if they feel that they are contributing positively. They will, in turn, tell others, and you will get better candidates to draw from when you hire. You also will have more loyal customers when they know they can shop where they are respected and will be treated fairly. As is the case with most of us, we just want to buy our products and go home. If we meet a bump along the way, we are happy if we can get it behind us and move on. Few are ready to throw everything away over a simple mishap.

Let me go on to say that this principle is not just for a retailer. If you are in a civic organization, school, professional office, church, or any other group, it is imperative that you keep the chain of command intact.

The other critical place is in the home. Today, we have a mixed-up society with nearly every combination of adults and children imaginable. We have different parents and stepparents, along with mixed races, genders, and so forth. It becomes absolutely mandatory that we have a hierarchy of authority in place and that we maintain it. If not, we will have children who will run from one authority to the other to get what they want. Dad says one thing. They don't like the answer, so they go to Mom. Or Mom says one thing, and they don't like the answer, so they go to Dad.

The combinations become endless if there is not an order that is being maintained, and if one authority doesn't upset the process and usurp the other, kids will use every type of leverage they can—"You're not my dad,""You're not my mom, "and so on. Better yet, the authorities in the house need to be in complete one accord and on the same page.

Sam Walton was exactly right that day in the parking lot when he impacted this young upstart with "don't break the chain of command," a lesson that has been very useful in life.

CHAPTER 7

Just Keep Yelling!

*My boss says I intimidate
the other employees,
so I just stared at him
until he apologized.*

IT WAS 1979, AND I WAS IN GRADUATE school in Portland, Oregon. Every student in my class had to do an extracurricular project. The project had to be outside the scope of any one academic class that we were taking and had to be a service project to our community. I decided to do a thirty-minute documentary. I had never produced any type of media project, and I was excited about taking on the endeavor. Besides, I had a friend who lived back east, and he had taken radio and television production in college. I could always draw on his wealth of knowledge wherever I ran short, which was most everywhere!

After about six months, I had a script, some boxes of slides, and a short three-minute movie clip that I had produced. Now all I needed was to put everything together and find a narrator to do the script. Since I had done some radio and television before, I thought I would just knock that out at a local radio station and I would be on my way.

One night I was talking to my previously mentioned friend, and he pointed out that it would be better if I could get someone else to do the narration. He thought a professional who wasn't attached to the project would give it a fresher quality. I agreed but didn't have anyone in mind or the money to spend. After all, I was a married graduate student, working two jobs and struggling. He said he would look for someone if I could be patient. I agreed and put everything on the back burner. I was on break between semesters and had plenty of other things that I needed to do.

One day I got a call from my friend who was at a college in Kankakee, Illinois, helping to produce a piece for another project of his. As we talked, he asked if I had gotten my project narrated. I told him that it wasn't on my priority list right now. He then told me he had a narrator at the studio where he was and that he could do the narration if I could be there by the next afternoon.

NEVER EXPECTED

Wow! That would be awesome, but I was in West Virginia, and he was five hundred miles away in Illinois. Well, I talked it over with my wife, and we decided that since my mother lived only about thirty-five miles from Kankakee, we could go up and have the narration done. And then we could visit my mother.

We were off that day, and we were ready for narration at about two o'clock that next afternoon. Oddly enough, the man who was going to do the narration was a minister and traveling speaker, and we shared the same first nickname, "Chuck." We met and shared a few things, and then I went over the script and the concept. We headed into the recording area, and we all took our places.

As Chuck began to record, I followed along with my copy of the script. He began, and I was so excited that this man was doing our script. It was just unimaginable that someone of his caliber was going to be doing this documentary. As I listened and followed along, he progressed to the second paragraph.

I yelled, "Stop!" I raced into the studio. "Chuck, could you read this part with a little more emphasis on this particular word?" I pointed to the script.

He graciously agreed, and we all took our places again. As the action started, he began, and I watched. He got to another spot about halfway through the same paragraph.

I yelled, "Stop!"

55

We went through the same process as before, and again he graciously agreed to make the suggestive changes in the emphasis and tone.

As he continued to make his way through the script, I continued to interrupt, yelling "Stop!" and requesting that he change emphasis in various parts. Finally (thank God) he stopped me after about the fourth or fifth interruption.

He very calmly looked at me, as I came back into the studio, and said, *"All emphasis is no emphasis!"*

Wow! Talk about a light going on. It was humbling and rewarding. I will be the first to tell you that this is not an easy principle to accept, apply, appreciate, or accomplish. In fact, it may be the most difficult of any I have learned. It can drain you of every ounce of energy and discipline you have.

Imagine a close friend who you get along famously with when suddenly he has a disagreement with you over some petty point of contention. Soon you are dismayed at his persistence in the matter, and you begin to lose it. Your voice raises, and then you are yelling and yelling. Usually the shouting is to get attention.

You are not really mad at your closest friend, but you are trying to get him to stop and hear you. The problem is that he has turned you off and is responding to the yelling, not to the point.

Do you get that? No. You just keep locked in on your

path and refuse to take and accept the limitation of your approach. If you have ever been around a person who is always saying that he loves this person and that person but truly can't stand the person that he says he loves, you realize that he is a lot of noise with no substance.

How about the person who always has an attitude? He is always angry and unappreciative. Then there is the person who is always complaining or sad or has to be right. This constant extreme level of anything detracts from the importance.

What about a different situation? How about the person who uses calmness and not yelling? Years ago, I was the women's volleyball coach at a nearby high school. I had a team that had some pretty good athletes at the time, but I was becoming a bit frustrated at not being able to bring them up to their potential.

Day after day, the assistant coach and I would go through the practice, planning, changing, and improvising, and still saw small, meager results. I refused to get excited and tried to always remain calm with the team.

My approach was to not come across as a bully to these young women. My continued emphasis on calmness had become complacency, mediocrity, and uninspiring to the team. Suddenly there was no emphasis. I was in actuality emphasizing just what I didn't want to emphasize.

Finally one of the team members raised her hand in a

meeting and asked, "Why don't you ever yell at us and get on our case when we do something wrong?"

I had not been applying the principle. I was still doing what I had done years before in the studio. This time it was in reverse. I wasn't yelling. I was constantly quiet with no emphasis, but the result was the same.

Nonstop badgering, whether it is loud or soft, gets the same results. Other areas can show the same result all the time. You know how you start watching a movie channel and they come up with a selection of movies that no one else is showing, maybe all mystery or romance movies. You think that this is great, along with several other people. Suddenly their ratings go off the chart, and they start making more and more of the same thing. The problem is that every movie has the same plot with a different setting. They are all good, mind you, but very much repetitive. Finally the whole concept that first drew you in has now become boring and uninviting, so you quit watching as much. Soon you quit watching at all and find another fresh channel you like.

All emphasis just became no emphasis. The channel owners wanted to emphasize a particular theme and did, so much, that the very thing they were trying to get across fell on deaf ears. If you really appreciate the point you want to make, you have to make it appreciative. Therefore, you have to give it honesty and color.

Advertisers understand this concept. Walt Disney was a master at this idea. He would design his movies with a crescendo of laughter and then a serious sadness. Up and down the viewer would go while through the whole movie he was taking you to one dramatic conclusion.

By the end of the movie, you walked away with a deep appreciation for how you were impacted by what you had learned. The ending was always happy. The idea of making the truth that he wanted you to grasp and making it appreciative is what built his company.

If he had used the approach to just pound the idea over and over, it would have been counter- productive. The approach has to be to know what you want to communicate and how to get the results you want. Applying the principle of varied emphasis has to be foundational, which will end in accomplishment. Accomplishment of such a principle requires great discipline. You can never yell too loud, and you can never be continually soft.

Case in point was my grandfather. I never heard him yell at anyone. He knew how to make emphatic exclamations with a raise in his voice. He also knew how to be quiet when necessary and how to be completely silent. He seemed to always know how to put the right emphasis on the matter. It sounds so easy but requires a lot of practice.

Chuck Millhuff understood this principle that all emphasis is no emphasis early in his career. I am sure it is one of the reasons he became a master communicator in his preaching, speaking, and narrations. No doubt, it is one of the reasons that the principle, he shared, made such an impression on me.

CHAPTER 8

I Didn't Get It. I Can't Have It. I Want It Now!

My job is secure. No one else wants it.

IN TRYING TO PREPARE FOR THIS CHAPter, I really had to do a lot of research and soul-searching. I kept thinking, *"What would be the best approach to illustrate what I believe may be the most revolutionizing principle of our lives?"* Now they are all important, and there are a few more to go in this book, but this next one has its tentacles in every phase of our thinking, speech, and belief system. What I came up with is a passage from Genesis to illustrate this principle. It is about the original sin, the

Garden of Eden, Eve the woman, Adam the man, and, of course, that old devil, the serpent.

Before I get there, let me tell you how I came across this concept. It was a hot afternoon in a little building at a used car lot at a new car dealership. I was working as a used car salesman. I worked with another salesman who was probably twice my age and had a very soft, pleasant manner about himself. He was one of those people you meet and think, *"Why is this guy doing this?"*

He came across as a teacher, philosopher, or some other type of educator. We would sit and talk. He always had something to say that would sort of blow you away. And it always got a delayed reaction from its target, which in this case was usually me.

About midmorning one day, onto the lot walked a customer. It was my turn, so I got up and headed out to greet the person. I went through the usual acknowledgements and niceties and then proceeded to match the person up with a particular automobile. Suddenly I said something that got this person upset, and she seemed to have immediate disdain for me and then wanted to take off. I was left in a whirlwind and couldn't grasp what had happened.

As I walked back to the little building, I kept going over what had just happened. It was very puzzling. I just couldn't get my mind around the results. I kept thinking

NEVER EXPECTED

that I had lost a sale and that I must not be cut out for this kind of work. I thought that maybe I had pushed too hard or said something that might have hit a nerve about something that I wasn't aware of. I was being filled with insecurity in my abilities and my self-image.

As I came into the building, Dan, the other salesman I mentioned earlier, asked what had happened. I began to explain the incident and said as soon as I tried to match the customer with an automobile that I thought would work, she just got rather irate, berated me, and took off.

Dan, in his very subtle and controlled way looked at me, and said, "Well, you made her feel insecure, and you know what insecurity does?"

Pause! Of course I thought I knew what insecurity does. I really didn't know where he was going with this, so I kept quiet.

Then he proceeded to tell me, "Insecurity breeds contempt."

Hmm! I thought, "I *am not sure I had ever thought of it that way.*"

Then he proceeded to give the rest of his undaunted wisdom. "And it demands control."

What! I had never heard anything like that. I had taken numerous psychology classes, and those definitions were never put with insecurity.

I politely said, "I had never quite looked at it that way."I

63

proceeded to complete the rest of the day with that peculiar concept constantly going through my mind.

Over the course of the next several years, I kept looking at different incidences where that wisdom seemed to come up over and over, and it always appeared to be true. Then I decided to break down and do some research to see if it would hold up in a more challenging scrutiny. That's what brings me to our Genesis passage. Not because that is the ultimate expression of the principle—life itself is that—but because it gives the perfect description. Okay, here we go.

Adam is given the control of the garden and told that he is to name everything. He is put in the garden, and it is said that in the midst of the garden there were put two trees. One was the Tree of Life; the other was the Tree of Knowledge, (*of good and evil*). So here is man (Adam) put into the garden to take care of it, but God tells him that he is free to eat of anything except the Tree of the Knowledge of Good and Evil because "when you eat of it, you will surely die (Genesis 2:17)."

Now in the very next verse, God says, "It is not good for the man to be alone, let us make a helpmate for him (Genesis 2:18)." Of course that helpmate is Eve. Now they are the happy couple until one day they come across a serpent who was more cunning than any other animal in the field. The serpent then proceeds to get into a conversation with Eve.

He asks a question. "Is it true that God has said you shall not eat of any tree of the garden?" So right off, he initiates a falsity, the beginning of the insecurity.

So the woman answers, "God said that we can eat of the fruit of the trees of the garden but of the fruit of the tree which is in the middle of the garden, God has said, 'You shall not eat of it, nor shall you touch it, lest you die.'"

You see how the account of what God said has already become convoluted. The serpent has twisted the truth to inject an element of insecurity, and now Eve responds to the serpent's misinterpretation and puts her own twist on the truth because she is feeling the insecurity. Let's keep going.

Now the serpent has to throw another wrench in the works. "You shall not surely die, for God knows in the day that you eat of it, your eyes will be opened, and you shall be as God, knowing good and evil."

Suddenly everything changed. She saw the fruit of the tree as good for food and pleasant to the eye. She saw that the tree was desirable to make one wise and that God's credibility was in question. *Perhaps God just told us certain things because He didn't want us to become as wise as He,* she probably thought.

She ate of it and then gave it to Adam, and he ate of it. Their whole perspective of life was changed, and their perspective of God and the serpent were changed as well.

If you remember in a previous chapter, we discussed the power of perspective.

All of this change comes about because the serpent played on the fear of the woman. Let me say that this is not a gender issue, nor am I trying to make it a religious issue. It is really a relationship issue. I am just illustrating how insecurity works.

Three things are involved in insecurity: anxiety, confidence, and personal fear. Let me say that all insecurity is fear based. There is fear when one is open to threat, be it danger of intrusion or the inability to protect one's self. Then there is the fear of personal failure. The fear of both physical vulnerability and personal are extremely forceful drives that can change our perspective of who are we, how we feel, and what we believe our capabilities are.

In our case above, Eve was thrown the task of believing the serpent that confused the mandate from only one tree to any tree. That is how insecurity is implanted through falsities, lies, accusations, and distortions. All carry with them the element of providing insecurity through fear and doubt. The serpent's challenge was to take what God had said, form it into a question based on a misinterpretation, and express it with an element of truth, with a conclusion of a lie.

Eve had to determine if she heard God correctly with a number: any, one, or all. Her confidence in God and

NEVER EXPECTED

herself was immediately called into play. Once you get on that path, you are already in the transport of insecurity. Remember the old adage, "Stop, look, and listen"? She needed to do those things and then refer to truth. I will come back to that later.

The next step is to cause anxiousness. Now we all have a certain propensity to be anxious. We sometimes call it anticipation or expectation, but more often, those things are actually anxiousness. Eve is pushed to respond and, of course, why. She responds by putting her own little twist on the matter. She replies to the serpent that they were not supposed to eat or touch the tree in the middle of the garden.

Now that is not what God said. He said that there were two trees in the midst of the garden, not one, but there was one that they were not to eat of. Touch was not in the rhetoric. She was already adding to the dialogue to cover her insecurity of confidence. She was uneasy and tried to alter the outcome (definition of anxiety).

Next enters the accusation. Surely you won't die. But that's what God said. No, He just knows that when you eat of the tree, you will be like Him. So there is a redefinition of terms. This is a common practice in debating. If you can slip in a new definition of terms and get the other side to accept it, you have just changed the playing field and the leverage in your favor.

In other words, the Serpent, points out that God is hiding something from them and they should get it, because then they will be as smart as He is. A powerful drive is to tell someone that he has been told a lie and the reason is to keep him in the dark. That is a great motivator, and the serpent used it to perfection. He stripped Eve of her confidence, built up her anxiousness, put the leverage in his favor, and then pushed her into personal fear. Now comes, the ultimate accomplishment.

After the serpent has done all of his damage, insecurity has been bundled up, and the explosion happens. She now gets contempt for God. She is convinced that God had lied to her to keep her from being like Him. God must have played her for a fool and told her that idea of dying from eating the very thing that would actually make her smarter was to keep her from knowing the truth.

Eve must have thought, *"What a contemptible God He must be." I will show Him and just take that fruit and become wise.* In other words, "I will get control of this situation right now. Oh, by the way, Adam, here you eat too, and we will both become wiser."

So her contempt was elevated. She demanded control of the situation and decided to be compassionate on the way to that control by offering this miracle fruit to her husband. From then on, everything changed … and not necessarily for the better.

Insecurity clouds our perspective. Remember in the earlier chapter I mentioned how perspective is power. It is not really knowledge as much as it is perspective. Insecurity gives us a different perspective, and that changes our direction. Another biblical account will show you what I mean. I use this one because it has one of the same leading characters repeating his same tactics and is a New Testament version of an Old Testament truth.

In Matthew 4, Jesus has gone into the wilderness after His baptism and has been on a forty-day fast. In this weakened condition, that old serpent, the devil, confronts Him. The devil tries the exact same tactic on Jesus as was tried on Eve in the garden but gets quite different results.

Jesus is tempted three times. First, the tempter tempts him to question His genealogy and authority. "If you are the Son of God, tell these stones to become bread." (Matthew 4:3). This is quite a temptation to someone who has not eaten for forty days. It also would play on an individual's confidence, especially in a weakened state, and if He could really change the stones into something to eat, that would undoubtedly be the ultimate temptation.

What is important is how it was handled. Jesus didn't take the bait. He instead referred the accusation to the truth. "Man does not live by bread alone" (Matthew 4:4). In other words, "You are not going to get me off my mission. I am focused on the *truth* and not leaving the path.

You cannot make me feel insecure. I have confidence in my path."

Second, the devil took Jesus to the high point of the temple. He quoted the Word of God and said, "If thou be the Son of God, cast thyself down: for it is written, He shall give his angels charge concerning thee, and in their hands, they shall bear thee up, lest at any time thou dash thy foot against a stone" (Matthew 4:5-6). The tempter was playing on Jesus' personal fear. But again the reference was to the truth. Jesus answered with another quote from the same source, the Word of God. "He should not tempt the Lord God" (Matthew 4:7). Again the temptation and attempt to build insecurity failed. Jesus did not develop any contempt for God or his own position. Again there had been no redefinitions to force Jesus onto another path, as was with Eve.

Third, the tempter tried to build anxiety by showing Jesus the kingdoms of the world and offering them to him. He was pointing out that he (Satan) had all of this power and possessions and that if Jesus would just submit to him, he would give Him all of these things. In essence, he was saying, "You don't have all that you believe God has given you. God doesn't have all of the power and the wealth like you thought, but I do. I can give it to you."

Again, that didn't work. The tempter was referred to the truth. Then saith Jesus unto him, "Get thee hence, Satan:

for it is written, thou shalt worship the Lord thy God, and him only shalt thou serve."

(Matthew 4:10). Finally the tempter left, but he did return, only to be defeated once again at the end of Jesus' life. The point here is that truth is the deterrent to insecurity.

In all three cases, the tempter was trying to make Jesus feel insecure in His position, relationship, and possessions and power. In all three cases, the tempter tried to get Jesus to bring about a slight redefinition of perspective of each passage. Insecurity always manifests in those three areas of our lives and is often given access through the redefining of terms or concepts. We open the door and give it an invitation when we have doubt, worry, and fear.

Often our doubt is based on misunderstandings or miscommunications. Perhaps we read into a statement that was made through an imagined discontent or sarcasm that wasn't intended, but we perceived it. It could even be hearing a word that was pronounced incorrectly. These are easy things to happen and often down the line start an avalanche of problems. It also could be something that someone deliberately told to you to lead you astray. Maybe it was something you heard or read and it was wrongly communicated.

In today's world of social media and unlimited sources of information, we are often inundated with bits of knowledge that must be researched heavily and then scrutinized before we act. We have had whole movements started out of one single twisted fact, redefining of a term, or loose accusation.

Worry brings another type of insecurity, that of great uncertainty. We become frantic when someone is supposed to be somewhere and they are late. We get very upset when the thing we had the greatest confidence in disappoints us.

Suddenly when this happens, we start to move chaotically and clamor to bring resolution to the issue. We seem to pull out all stops to correct the mystery of why this thing, which we had the greatest confidence in, has brought our great expectations down to the pit.

Then there is the fear. Fear is really based in every facet of insecurity. The fear is the motivator. Worry and doubt bring the question of insecurity, but fear gets us to act. It is not enough to bring doubt or worry. These are not always bad elements in and of themselves. Doubt can help the scientist to push to new discoveries. Worry can cause one to exhibit immense sympathy and even empathy.

When they are mixed with the element of fear, they become a devastating factor of destruction. Fear causes both worry and doubt to run out of control. Without hesitation, there is born in the midst of the incident an insatiable desire to have contempt for the person, place, or thing that has brought this fear into their life. This contempt is then mixed with manipulation and force to stop this imagined onslaught of events or rhetoric that is making one feel insecure.

Now the whole experience gets reduced to breeding contempt (multiplying the contempt over and over) and demanding control. Of course, the ultimate irony is that those two things do not and will not bring security. Instead they bring just the opposite. They keep multiplying the insecurity until it becomes like an uncontrollable vine with its tentacles embedded in every facet of our life. One begins to develop paranoia, obsessive behaviors, anger, and other unwanted personality traits.

When we develop a healthy view, of exactly who we are, where we are going, and what our real capabilities are, we can walk in confidence; without anxiety or fear. We can instead walk in security. Security is based on a whole different set of values. Security never has contempt for the things that are attacking it. Rather it has confidence in the dynamics of the truth. The truth is the stabilizer, which is the standard that cannot be shaken, thwarted, or dissolved.

Security never demands control but commands control. Again truth reigns. Truth stands alone at the pinnacle, and everything else has to measure up to it. Security, confidence, stability, assurance, and fearlessness are all based on truth. Truth is the motivator of security and leadership.

If you look at leaders throughout history, many were leaders because they brought fear and insecurity to the people. Many of the Caesars of early Rome and others brought a deep insecurity to their followers and demanded control to the point of imprisonment or even death. The leaders who brought liberation and freedom brought a sense of security and confidence to those who had been held in bondage. Truth brings freedom. Before I go any farther, I need to show one more aspect of insecurity and how the truth brings security.

Most insecurity is housed in a false security or the belief of security that is in actuality insecurity.

Let's say that a person has a belief that all farmers are bad and dangerous to be around. (Remember this is only an example). One day a farmer sees an insecure person. We will call him IP in a troubled situation. With great compassion, the farmer rushes to help IP. IP is hesitant to accept any help from the farmer. Why? Accepting help means that IP's anger, disdain, and preconceived bias would be in question.

Suddenly the comfort of all of IP's belief system is brought into question. Essentially the balloon of the false security of a wrong conclusion has to be popped. This means IP has to become vulnerable to the truth, which puts IP in a very insecure position, trust. In order to move to security, he has to give up his position of false security and pass through anticipated insecurity to get to security. (Whew! Did you get that?)

This can be a frightening journey. Many people are so fearful of having to face truth that they willfully decide to remain in their false security and the bondage that it provides rather than make the liberating trek to truth and freedom.

To wrap up, let's go back to our example. Eve was made to be doubtful of her relationship to God and told that God was not really truthful with her, that He had a hidden motivation. So she operated on a lie. Jesus, on the other hand, was very secure in His relationship with God (His father), and the devil's ploy of trying to redefine things could not sway Him.

When a leader is very secure in whom he is, people want to follow him. His demeanor draws people to his path. He is given control and never has to demand control. When someone is constantly having contempt for others and always ranting and raving for control, know that they are operating out of deep insecurity. That approach is sure to have dire consequences along the way.

When things are not going your way, remember my old friend **Dan Crowder** and that insecurity breeds contempt and demands control. Get back on path and look for truth. Embrace it, and you will walk in security, not insecurity.

—

CHAPTER 9

How Much Longer Until We Get There?

The wall was just ahead, but I ignored the warning signs and picked up the speed.

IF YOU HAVE EVER BEEN TRAVELING with children, you know that their question repeated over and over until you reach your destination is, "How much longer till we get there?" It seems simple enough, and we often dismiss it with little or no regard. Well, one day that phrase took on a whole new meaning for me.

It was a hot, muggy afternoon in July, about 1972. I was traveling back from Little Rock, Arkansas, listening to the radio and trying to stay awake for the last fifty miles I had to travel. I kept thinking, *"How much longer until I get there?"* I was tired and hungry, and I was on a partly finished back road. Travel was both fast and slow, so I was listening to the radio as much as I could to try to stay awake. I would flip from one station to the other, trying to find something that would come in clear and hold my interest. It's not easy in the mountains of northern Arkansas and southwest Missouri.

Suddenly I caught a station that I believe was coming from Little Rock, Arkansas, and it was as clear as a bell. As a plus, it was a talk radio program, which at the time was hard to find. You generally got a music station that didn't play a great selection.

Well, here I was listening to some radio host interviewing someone I had never heard of before, and they were talking about a whole bag of ideas, such as, "What do you do when someone lies to you? What do you think a hypocrite is?" It was just a lot of mixed questions that seemed to have no direction; sometimes though, that kind of thing can hold your attention, especially when you are a captive audience. Just about the time I was going to look for another station, the conversation changed, and I became locked into the dialogue.

The interviewer began asking his guest to give his definition of some different words. The guest responded with some unusual answers. Surprisingly, the word *fanatic* came up. Well, there was a short pause and then a response I never expected.

The definition from the dictionary for fanatic is, "A person filled with excessive and single-minded zeal, especially for an extreme religious or political cause."A small variation of that definition was what I was expecting, particularly with an emphasis on the religious part because that is the part that usually gets exploited. However, what I heard was really enlightening.

"A fanatic", he responded, "is someone who has lost sight of his objective and doubled his effort."

Now that is simple enough, but if I may, let me share a little depth as to what I see that meaning being in relation to the dictionary meaning.

The first part we need to examine is the last part of the dictionary quote, for a religious or political cause. The truth is that we have fanatics for all kinds of causes. It's just the political and particularly the religious ones that get the greatest attention. There are also fanatics in sales, business, antique collection, food preparation, teaching, and so on. The one thing I have noticed is that they are all filled with zeal.

Zeal is not a bad thing on the contrary; it is a great motivator. If you are an employer or an employee, zeal is a great attribute. However, the principle must take into account that when one becomes fanatical, his zeal can become mixed with chaos, confusion, and calamity. This happens, especially when it becomes excessive. That is what causes the "doubling his effort" part.

Often when one becomes truly fanatical, his effort becomes relentless. He seems to be unwilling to stop at any cost. Suddenly there is a desire to make any sacrifice and pay any amount to reach his goal. His zeal turns to obsession.

Once obsession begins to take over, a second problem, confusion, sets in. The confusion is a type of dyslexia of reason. What is right is wrong; what is wrong is right. The change in reasonableness versus unreasonableness becomes virtually indistinguishable to the person with the obsession. A blind spot is birthed, and only he can see the obstruction and not the obstacle on the other side of the blind spot. It is like backing out of your driveway and only being able to see the doorpost of your car and not the other car that you are about to sideswipe.

So now the fury of the obsession is all that is visible. It is the only right that can be seen or even tolerated. From this point on, the fanatic can only see this one point of view and nothing else. All information about the subject is filtered through the blind spot and processed to fit the warped view. No amount of reason can change this. In fact, the more reason and truth that is brought into the issue,

NEVER EXPECTED

the more the blind spot grows. And the more it is accepted as fact, even though it is not based on any fact. Thus reasonable becomes unreasonable, and unreasonable appears to be very reasonable.

Next becomes a quest only to prove his being right, whether it is right or wrong.

The only issue now is to reach "a goal," not "the goal." The increased effort obscures the original goal. The goal to do something helpful and meaningful is behind the blind spot and is no longer on the table of contents. What matters now is just to get his point of view into operation.

At this point, all effort is made to reach the goal that is no longer there. Sight of the original objective is lost and not possible to bring into view. The only thing that can be seen is to make more effort so the selfish desire and ideology can be known, which has become the blind spot. Effort is doubled; objective is lost.

It is as if one is going down a dead-end street, about to hit a wall of stone. So he steps on the accelerator to get there faster. Every warning sign is ignored, and all that matters is reaching the blind spot faster. The person has literally lost sight of his objective and doubled his effort. He has become fanatical.

To avoid this, a person must regularly stop and check where he is and make sure that his goal is still based on fact. He still has a clear view of the original vision, and nothing along the way has changed his course. If you are open to the facts and sound logical reasoning, it will help you to keep from getting the blind spots. Where someone has the problem is accepting facts that challenge his point of view and long-held established beliefs.

It is never easy to admit that a belief you held all of your life or was taught to you by some personal hero could be wrong. Sometimes you embrace the truth that you have always believed, though it may only be an opinion and not a fact at all. When the fact comes along, the opinion is exposed for what it is, regardless of how much you want to believe it is right. If a person will turn to factual truth and be willing to use that as the measuring stick, the possibility of becoming a fanatic will be slim at best. Without a factual truthful measuring device, we all would be on an exhausting roller-coaster ride, going up and down and in and out of one exasperating experience after another, always in a pressure situation resulting in a calamity.

CHAPTER 10

Success: Where Is It? And How Do I Get It?

There are two rules for success:
(1) Don't tell all you know.

WHERE IS SUCCESS, AND HOW DO I GET it? Just a straightforward question that everyone, I believe, on the planet has asked at least once in his life. I know that I had asked that question numerous times as a kid, a young man, and even as an adult. It is like those questions we are told that everybody wants an answer to: Who am I? Where am I going? What is my purpose? They are all great questions, and all need answers. Well, so does the question of success.

DR. CHARLES FRANGELLA

Let me start off by saying that true success is different for everyone because each person has a different concept of what success is; a lawyer, baker, or candlestick maker all have their own concept of success for their personal life, and expectations. However, the elements of getting success are the same. It takes the same qualities to achieve success for the scientist who is working on the most complicated microbiology discovery as it takes for the young boy or girl trying to master a game of sandlot baseball. I will tell you that the principles are what I found from observation of many people over a period of many years because of asking that question many times.

Back in the 1970s, I moved from Illinois to Missouri. I went to a place I had never been before to visit some friends. I went with every intention to move there but was prepared to return to Illinois if things didn't work out.

I made the trek of about nine hours with just my truck, a few hand tools, and thirty-five dollars. That was it, all I had. I had left -10-degree weather and a very good job (cold turkey) during a time when I had been laid off and went with the determination that hopefully I wasn't coming back. When I reached my destination, it was late, but I talked for awhile to my friends and then went straight to bed.

The next day, one of my friends took me to lunch. While there, in this little local restaurant, he introduced me to a local contractor. Before our conversation had ended, I had a job laying some block for this newly found contractor friend. Wow! I was elated. I had been here for less than a day, and I had a job.

Within months I had accomplished so much. I had numerous friends and business acquaintances, a second business, and some rental property. It was amazing to me, but I was still asking the question, "How do I get success?"

I was asking the question because I had achieved a lot but didn't perceive what I had achieved or how I had gotten it. All I saw was work and more work. That didn't spell success. In essence, I wanted to know principles that I could duplicate over and over and in other venues. Success in construction or real estate is not the same as success in personal relationships, teaching school, or some other pursuit, or so I thought. How do I get the secret? How can I use some magical formula to conquer any goal that I might have?

As a twenty-five-year-old, that was the ingredient I was searching for, the hidden potion I could sprinkle on any endeavor of my heart's desire and it would become a success. Wouldn't that be the most amazing find? No need for any special gifts or education. Just apply this miraculous idea or concept to whatever I want to do and presto! Success! Actually nothing comes easily, but it can be simple. Just like some things aren't necessarily right, but they may be true; these are two nuggets I learned from my older brother.

Well, for the next few years I was in business and out of business. Then I was in school and out of school. I moved around a lot. I lived in a couple of countries, worked at a lot of different jobs, and went through some personal heartaches, but never seemed to experience any kind of success.

Then one day while listening to the radio, I heard someone talking, and it hit me. Suddenly I knew what was wrong and how to correct it. Now let me tell you that the person didn't say the principles I am going to share, but he sure opened my eyes to them. I want to add that you may read these principles and think they are too simple. Let me warn you that they are simple, but they are not easy.

The first reality that hit me that day was the need to be responsible. Now, most of us know the common concept of being responsible. You have an obligation to do something or have control over something. Then there is the other type of responsibility, which is to be the primary cause of something, so as to be blamed or credited for it. Then there is that which you are capable of being trusted with and morally accountable for your behavior.

I had always thought that I could be trusted, but could I be diligent, to follow something all the way through and take the responsibility for the outcome, whether it was positive or negative? I had to wake up to the fact of the disaster that may follow. My effort may just fall on my shoulders. In the following years, I noticed that people who are truly successful in different areas of their lives have this quality. They are willing to stand up and take credit for their decisions, even if they fail and have dire consequences.

This is not taking false humility or trying to take someone else's blame. That position fits a whole different category and doesn't belong in this realm. This is about the person who can be responsible, trusted, and valued. Being responsible is a two-edged sword. It involves being diligent and accountable in all areas. I will be coming back to this principle later. Hold that thought.

The second reality that shoved me in the corner and said "take notice" was discipline. There are several meanings for discipline, but I want to primarily discuss the one that has to do with oneself. This definition says to train oneself to do something in a controlled and habitual way. There is another part of the verb definition, to train to obey rules of a code of behavior and to use punishment to correct disobedience.

Now, let's look at these two together. I must then train myself to do something in a controlled and habitual way so I will obey rules or principles and develop a code of behavior. To accomplish this goal, I must be willing to set up a system of some type of punishment to correct my disobedience. Sounds horrible, but it isn't. No one likes to do this, and yet we do it all the time. Remember, I stated earlier that these elements of success are just that. They don't discriminate, so you can use them for good or bad. You can be successful doing something that is good and beneficial, or you can do something that can be horrible. Oddly, the same rules apply.

One often develops a discipline of a bad habit such as eating disorders, substance abuse, deceptions, lying, and so forth. That type of discipline comes easy, and one is more than willing to do what it takes to achieve his goal. If he tries to apply the same rules for good in his life, it seems much more difficult and not nearly as desirable.

If you want success in your personal relationships, business, education, or anything else, you have to develop discipline. The rewards are just as good, but they come more slowly. When you are chasing the bad addictions, you can put all your energy, effort, and focus into it, but when it is a good addiction that you need to nurture, it becomes more challenging. The visibility of results is slower.

Think of preparing soil for a garden. You put in the same discipline whether weeds or your vegetables grow. The weeds, however, take very little effort. The vegetables, on the other hand, require a lot of time and effort, and it takes a great deal of time before you begin to see the fruit of your labor, but the preparing of the soil was the same.

Let's move on to the next element. I will be coming back to discipline.

The third element that boldly got my attention was the concept of sacrifice. Now, sacrifice here is not the idea of putting an animal on the altar. It is about giving up something. It is about giving something valued for the sake of something else, regarded as more important or worthy.

To truly be successful, sacrifices are imperative. It is about making choices. Making hard choices is a necessary step if you are going to progress. Sometimes choices are not just difficult but often are gut-wrenching. They are decisions that seem to tear you apart, and you cannot see the logic at all. However, sacrifice is uncaring and unemotional. It is based simply on the best choice to reach the goal. There is never having a warm fuzzy feeling or a lightning bolt of epiphany. It is just what it takes and nothing else. It is based on what is needed to bring about complete satisfaction to meet the requirements.

The choices have to be made, and ultimately it comes down to either-or. There is no pretty way. It would be great, if this element, were not a part of success, but in many ways, it is the most significant and most telling. This is usually the one element that causes most people to stumble and keeps success from ever materializing in their lives. Often when they get much older, they look back and realize their regrets for not being willing to make the necessary sacrifices in their lives.

Previously I mentioned that I would be coming back to the other elements, and this seems like the right place to do that. The reason sacrifice, discipline, and responsibility are united to success is in their emphatic codependency. Success, for any of us, is found throughout our lives and at many stages, both chronologically and experientially. Thus the picture looks like a three-legged stool with success being the seat and the three elements being the legs, but that is still too simple because all of the legs are interdependent of one another and two of the legs are needed to actually form the third leg. They are all needed, but two are intricately a part of the third. Let me explain.

The two legs—discipline and sacrifice—are components of responsibility. To truly be responsible, you must be trustworthy and accountable. One has to be able to make sacrifices and be disciplined. If you're not willing to make sacrifices, how will you ever hold yourself accountable? You may claim accountability, but will you make the sacrifice of all that it takes to claim full accountability, or will you stop short when the demand gets too great? To claim full accountability, you have to make the complete sacrifice.

Discipline is also a component because to be truly responsible, you must be trustworthy. To be trustworthy, you must discipline yourself to being habitual. People who

NEVER EXPECTED

exhibit weakness and are haphazard in their approach show that they are untrustworthy. Without showing routine and resolve, a person appears irresponsible.

The two legs of discipline and sacrifice are independent on their own but are necessary to form the third leg of responsibility. Therefore our stool is not really a stool but more of a towering sign that has two gigantic pillars of discipline and sacrifice that hold up another pillar of responsibility. Then in turn the three hold up the sign, "Success."

I have found from talking to others and observing others that all those who are successful—whether it be, in business, education, human relationships, marriage, science, writing, journalism, ministry, or anything else you can name—exhibit these three qualities. All three are necessary to hold up the sign. I might add that when they don't have anyone of these elements, true fulfilling success eludes them. As I mentioned earlier, they are simple but not easy. And the earlier you develop them, the quicker and easier you will experience success and the less heartache you will have.

CHAPTER 11

"I Have No Silver or Gold, But What I Have I Give"

*I inherited a lot of money.
It's been ten years, and
I'm still looking for it.*

THERE IS A PRINCIPLE THAT HAS probably been around since the beginning of the human race. It is something you are most likely familiar with, but I thought if I didn't include some variation of it in this book, I would be very amiss. Again I return to the Bible for the ultimate illustration. Here, we will see all of the components of this principle and the fullness of its impact on those involved.

In the opening of the book of 2 Kings, there are two prophets, Elijah and Elisha. Elijah is the senior prophet who has already established himself as a radical by defying the prophets of Baal, standing against King Ahab, and rejecting Queen Jezebel. In the midst of this, young Elisha desires to follow Elijah and wants only one thing, to receive a double portion of the spirit that is on Elijah.

When Elijah is taken away in a whirlwind, Elisha is standing near him, and Elijah's mantle (cape) falls from him. Elisha then picks up Elijah's mantle and cries out, "My father, my father." (II Kings 2:12) From that day forward, Elisha walks after the way of Elijah, and there is recorded an exact double amount of miracles performed by Elisha.

Now the point is not to have a Bible lesson, though it is a good one, but rather to refer to a long-standing principle that has literally been prevalent in every culture and era of the human race but is also quickly moving toward disappearance. It is the principle tradition of passing the mantle from one generation to the next. Again I say, "That is simple," but it is not necessarily easy.

The principle of "passing the mantle" is not just giving your son or daughter a piece of good advice, showing him how to change a tire or balance a checkbook. Although these skills are needed and often neglected, passing the mantle is passing an actual part of you. Your mantle is what makes you tick. Anyone can pass things along to another generation. Teachers, leaders, heroes, icons, friends, family, and enemies can all pass something. Some things are wanted; others are not.

But what the next generation needs is that part of you that has shaped you and made you into the person you are. It is a sum total of your life's experience and the values and principles that have motivated you and caused you to think the way you think and come to the conclusions that you draw. These things come from your cultural background, your everyday environment, and the mantle that was passed to you.

What seems to be lacking in today's world is that most people are afraid of the responsibility of a mantle. They are afraid they have nothing to offer because when they look back at themselves, they begin to see a lack of discipline, a deficiency of hard-core and life-changing values, and a depleted vault of morals. The mantle must have an abundance of those qualities that will actually overflow to the next generation.

We communicate in four basic concepts: rules and *regulations, policies, traditions, and desires.* The idea of passing a mantle is most widely transferred through the latter two. Traditions and desires communicate the essence of who we are. Traditions speak to our past, our ancestry, and the reoccurring events that we learned from and cherish.

To those near us or to those who hold us in esteem, these things speak to who we are and to others having confidence and trust in us.

Desires do much the same thing, except they are even more personal. Desires tell the other person that not only are these things what we like, but they are what we believe will be good for them. Every parent has desires for their children, parents, siblings, and spouses, even for friends and coworkers. The transparency of these ways of communicating opens us up and draws others to want to receive our mantle.

Elisha was surely not attracted to the lifestyle of Elijah or the turmoil and adversity that Elijah went through. He was drawn to the person who had a tradition of following God and a desire to show others how to follow God. Elisha wanted a double portion of that mantle.

The "passing of the mantle" comes in three stages.

The first is from commitment. It takes commitment from both parties. Normally this is strongest between family, that is, mother/daughter, father/son, brother/sister, and various other combinations. It has to be commitment that comes from deep desire and not a haphazard infatuation that may come and go. This commitment must be a willingness to sacrifice for one another and not allow for any diversion. Elijah repeatedly asked Elisha to wait at several different places, but Elisha refused and stayed the course

NEVER EXPECTED

because he was committed regardless of the adversity. Elijah was committed to Elisha from the very beginning.

When they joined together, Elijah immediately asked Elisha, "What shall I do for you before I am taken away?" (II Kings 2:9).

Elisha responded that he wanted to receive a double portion of Elijah's spirit. Elijah responded "Thou hast asked a hard thing: nevertheless, if thou see me when I am taken from thee, it shall be so unto thee: but if not it shall not be so." (II Kings 2:10). A double commitment is the key.

The second phase is the following. Once one person begins to follow, he must stay behind the person until the time that the mantle is passed. There is no rushing the process. You cannot alter the route. It must come to the rightful destination, or the fullness of the mantle is not complete. That is generally the downfall. Most people become tired and want to jump out and start out on their own. To do this is to ensure that you will not get the mantle. However, it is the responsibility of both parties. The leader must help the follower to keep following. That's why he is the leader. If either of these two things breaks, the passing will not happen. The journey takes two.

The third step is application. Again, this is a two-person part. When Elisha took the mantle, he went to the Jordan River, struck the water, and called out, "Where is the Lord God of Elijah?" (II Kings 2:14).

97

This act embodies the whole idea of passing the mantle. Elisha asked for a double portion of the spirit of Elijah, not just something of Elijah's. Elisha wanted the very essence of everything that Elijah was. He came to the point of division (Jordan means divided) and instantly challenged that confrontation. He was confident that he had the mantle. He didn't wimp around and struggle with useless introspection, questioning whether he should or shouldn't cross the river as he had seen Elijah. He just smote the waters and made a demand.

When we are going to pass a mantle, we must desire to pass the very best of our self. The one we are passing to must receive with a confidence that he has gotten the very best of us.

Today, things are often reduced to quick remakes, junk imitations, and inferior duplicates. It is a tendency to live our lives in such a fashion that when we go to pass something along, it often resembles a cheap version of that lifestyle. We must try to build quality of principles, values, and morals into ourselves for a legacy to pass along. We need to design our life in such a way that we will attract an "Elisha" to want to desire a double portion of what we have. We are never too old; nor is it ever too late for a turnaround. We should have a great desire to want to pass the mantle so the next generation can carry on that which made the previous generation great and will help to preserve the present generation.

We must be careful to cling to a solid remnant of core values, morals, and traditions of the past and preserve them for the future. In order to bring stability to our society and depth to our heritage, our goal should be to make a willing, responsible, and conscious effort at passing the mantle to our offspring or to someone who has pledged his respect for us. We must not allow someone else to step in and pass his mantle to the ones who are designed to receive our mantle.

CHAPTER 12

"Without It, We Would Be Most Miserable"

*Learn from yesterday,
live for today, and have
hope for tomorrow.*

HAVING FINISHED GRADUATE SCHOOL several years before, I had gone through some horrible situations that I wasn't sure I would survive, but I did. As is the case with graduations, you leave friendships that you have developed and hope to keep alive down through the years. Of course, usually life interrupts your plans, and friendships are put aside. In many cases, they are only to be remembered in a few very special melancholy moments.

However, thank God, a few friendships endure and last the rest of your life. So it was with me.

I have had a few friendships that I have developed along life's way that have nonetheless stuck with me for years, even to my lack of understanding as to why. I have been grateful for these friendships. At some of the most critical times in my life, I have been able to draw on them to help me get through the rough patches.

As I was saying, it had been several years since graduation, and I had just entered a vocation of which I had a lot of uncertainty. There was going to be a lot of pressure, stress, and demands that raised many questions. Sometimes no amount of schooling or even related types of experiences can prepare you for what you are about to face. I guess that's why life is designed to have interruptions that you would never expect along the way, to invoke principles and friendships so we can get through the next chapter of our lives. Well, I was coming into one of those times, so I called a friend who I knew could help.

Joe had left graduate school and moved to Green Bay, Wisconsin, the same time I left and moved to Charleston, West Virginia. Our paths were not similar in any way, but we were somehow at a comparable point. So I called him and asked about his situation in Green Bay. I knew that he had sometime before taken a small storefront church that had approximately thirty-five members, and

NEVER EXPECTED

under his leadership, its membership increased to approximately a thousand members. I considered that to be a huge accomplishment.

As we talked, he explained to me that the church was not new but had been in existence for a long time before he had come along. I was shocked.

"Really," I said. "What did you do to create such growth?"

He responded, "I prayed, and the answer came: give them hope."

That was so simple but yet so meaningful. It was the water to a person in the desert or food to the hungry. To give a person, group, or anyone something that will meet their exact need is what we all want and all want to give.

Think of it in a different context. In the United States, we have an election every four years to select a leader. Campaigns are run, millions of dollars are spent, and slurs and slogans are thrown out all to promote a candidate. Incumbents run on their past records, and new challengers run on future promises. If you look at the winners, it usually is the one who gives the people the most hope. It is not really the candidate who makes all the promises, but the one who instills real hope in the listener. If they can come up with a message that resonates with the listener, there is hope in the future with him. The listener has their vote. The same is true in every other facet of our lives, whether it be church, politics, or anything in between. If I may, let me break down this idea of hope, its strength, and the importance of this principle in your life.

Hope is a trust or confidence that you place in someone or something to have a future beneficial result. It can be in a process, a person (someone you do or don't like), a plan, or an idea that you are certain will bring about a positive impact to your life. Thus, hope is one of those words that is defined by its use as a noun and a verb, but its effect; is a mixture of both. Hope can be either a negative or a positive. Some people develop a hope for the end of a marriage or to see something destroyed, while another has hope for the recovery of that same marriage or the hope that nothing will be destroyed. Hope then produces inspiration, motivation, and perspiration, without regard to moralization.

I want hope to inspire me and move me to look to future accomplishments with short- and long-term goals. I also want to be someone who can duplicate that same effect in others. To keep it for only me, would be to restrict the enormity of hope's potential. If I do that, it then becomes unfulfilling to me, and soon hope is lost. And I am in need of a fresh dose of hope's medicine to get myself back on track.

Joe was able to do that with his congregation. He was experiencing a new chapter in his life, and he needed hope that could keep him motivated through the difficulties and challenges of being a pastor of a small group of people, a group that had been hanging on and enduring for years. The people needed hope to continue going forward. They were being asked to put their trust in yet another person who might or might not take them somewhere. If the hope were not inspirational, they would all be living in disappointment, the people in their long-term routine and Joe in the realization that, if what he did didn't work, he didn't know where he would go from there.

But hope was inspiration to all to trust one another, anticipate different results, and overcome past failures. The inspiration then became excitement. But excitement isn't enough to get the job done. A lot of people get excited about a dream, plan, or brilliant idea, but they never move past the excitement stage. How many times have you heard someone say that he had such-and-such idea but he had never done anything about it? Then years later, someone came up with the same idea and made it happen. As I stated earlier, hope is also motivational.

Hope has the ability to move someone. When a person is lost in a myriad of troubles, doubts, or confusion, a spark of hope can completely change his perception. A person crossing the desert without any water suddenly sees an oasis. He doesn't just dream of the water that might be there, but he is motivated to take every last ounce of strength and apply it to reaching that miraculous site.

The inventor who has been struggling possibly for years sees one little change, and hope spurs him into a new test. In a relationship that has fallen on the rocks, the smallest word of kindness can be spoken, and one or both people begin to have hope, that things can be different. They make an effort to change their outlook and be more focused on a solution instead of adding to the problem.

What happens is that hope brings about a fresh perspective. Perspective is power. The power of hope is commitment. When hope is abundant, commitment becomes abundant. A person gets hope, and then he becomes motivated and committed. New horizons are viewed. New efforts are made. People begin to look at potential in place of lack of resources. The smallest seed becomes a great tree. It is no longer just what I have but is now the potential of what I have and the desire to extract that potential.

I think of my visit to Rome, Italy, some years ago. My first glimpse of the *Pieta*, one of Michelangelo's amazing sculptures, was created when he was only twenty-four years old. At this young age, he could look at a giant piece of marble and envision this beautiful resemblance of the Mother Mary holding the body of the crucified Christ. His hope of taking that piece of marble gave him the inspiration and motivation to take a chisel and hammer and make the first cut. There are numerous examples that I could use, such as Mount Rushmore or the Empire State Building.

NEVER EXPECTED

The list could go on and on, but there is another imperative part of hope, perspiration.

If hope were only good for inspiration and motivation, it would be good, but not really complete. Hope brings perspiration. Hope keeps a person working. It is hope that not only pulls you past the inspiring idea and the motivation to begin, but keeps you, continuing down the path in spite of yourself.

The people in the church and the pastor (**Joe Urcavich**, former chaplain of the Green Bay Packers) had to work through a lot of disappointments and changes of plans along the way. Undoubtedly there were disagreements, hurt feelings, and angry moments, but the hope of seeing a project come to completion got everyone through those moments. Everyone was willing to keep working in order to get to the finish line.

Michelangelo was willing to endure the cruel treatment that he suffered from the church leadership and the mockery from the people. He kept sweating in unbearable conditions so he could reach the finished product. George Washington Carver had to spend countless hours in a laboratory going through one test after another, often getting unsatisfactory results to finally get a conclusion. It is said that Thomas Edison had a thousand failures before he discovered the light bulb.

How many people have gone through hours and hours

of counseling before they resolved their differences and put their marriage back together, all because of hope? How many drug addicts had to go through several attempts at rehab before they finally found enough hope that convinced them they could have a better life? No one would endure such things without an inner drive of hope to reach fulfillment; Hope will give one excitement, hold them to commitment, and produce fulfillment.

This becomes the principle of principles. Giving hope becomes the one thing that we all need and should embrace. To pass along a hope that is inspirational to each and every person is an imperative that must be at the center of our mission in life. Being someone who brings hope to motivate others should become the directive of every endeavor. Being able to perspire and give others the desire to perspire in order to finish their dream should be the sacrifice that all of us are willing to make.

I only hope that this book was not only enlightening but was inspiring and passed along a hope to you and a desire to pass *hope* along to others.

ABOUT THE AUTHOR

DR. CHARLES FRANGELLA earned several degrees, including a master's degree in art and a PhD. He's written poetry, collaborated with Nashville song writers on lyrics, owned a restaurant and commercial real estate business, served on missions, was a school administrator, spent fourteen years as a pastor, and has been an adjunct professor at the University of Charleston and West Virginia University. He and his wife, Marcia, have lived in Ripley, West Virginia, for thirty years.

To Nell,

I have been blessed to have you in my life.

Charlie